ASIAPAC COMIC SERIES

P9-DVH-950

Origins of Chinese Festivals
中国节日的故事

Compiled by **Goh Pei Ki**
Illustrated by **Fu Chunjiang**
Translated by **Koh Kok Kiang**

ASIAPAC • SINGAPORE

ier

S PTE LTD

ɔad #04-06

ial Building

Singapore 389838

Tel: (65) 7453868

Fax: (65) 7453822

Email apacbks@singnet.com.sg

Visit us at our Internet home page

http://www.asiapacbooks.com

First published May 1997

Cover illustration by Fu Chunjiang

Cover design by Foo Hwee Sin

Body text in 8/9 pt Helvetica

Printed in Singapore by

Chung Printing

Publisher's Note

As a publisher dedicated to the promotion of works on Chinese culture and philosophy, we are pleased to bring you this graphic presentation of *Origins of Chinese Festivals* 中国节日的故事.

The Chinese people have a long history of civilization. Information about the origins of Chinese traditional festivals not only help us to understand the customs and everyday habits of the Chinese but also their rich cultural heritage. The reader will be intrigued to learn that many of the stories associated with Chinese festivals have evolved with the changes in the development of the Chinese civilization and as a consequence have become an integral part of the Chinese culture.

It is hoped that this book on the origins of the festivals and popular stories associated with them will help the reader to appreciate how the celebration of these festivals has helped the Chinese stick together as a race throughout their long history.

We would like to express our gratitude to Fu Chunjiang for his lively illustrations, Goh Pei Ki for her compilation, Dr Lee Cheuk Yin for writing the Preface, and Koh Kok Kiang for translating this volume and writing the Introduction. Our thanks, too, to the production team for putting in their best effort in the publication of this book.

Preface

Traditional festivals can be seen as a nation's cultural uniqueness and a by-product of civilization. The longer the nation's history, the more varied and richer are its festivals. The development of Chinese culture dates back some 4,000 years ago and as such, Chinese traditional festivals have come a long way. According to American scholar Professor Derk Bodde, some of the festivals observed by the Chinese, like the Lunar New Year 农历新年 and Winter Solstice 冬至, were already national festivals since as early as the Han Dynasty in the second century BC. As can be seen, festivals have been an integral part of Chinese culture for a very long time.

Festivals came about when humans lived together in groups in society and accepted certain customs through common practice. In the beginning, festive activities were shaped according to the wishes of the people and reflected their psychological needs. As time went on, a kind of tacit agreement was formed and it gave birth to an exclusive custom. The festival, as a whole, is a complex cultural feature which incorporates myths, beliefs, psychological inclinations and customs of the people. So an excellent way of understanding a particular nation's culture is to study its traditional festivals.

Traditional Chinese festivals are both varied in range and extremely colourful in quality. They can be grouped under three major categories: seasonal, historical or mythical, and religious. The Lunar New Year and Winter Solstice are examples of seasonal festivals. The Dragon Boat Festival 端午节 and Mid-Autumn Festival 中秋节 have strong historical or mythical undertones while the Hungry Ghost Festival 中元节 is a clear-cut religious affair. Depending on their individual characteristics, these festivals can also be categorized as single-purpose affairs or multi-faceted ones.

The former category is characterized by its limitation to one purpose. Examples are: the ancient Military Review Festival 阅兵节, Cold Food Feast 寒食节 and religious festivals like Buddha's Birthday 佛祖诞 and Goddess of Mercy's Birthday 观音诞. The activities centred on a single purpose. In the latter category, the activities are all-encompassing and diversified to reflect the festivals' multi-faceted characteristics. Take for example, the Lunar New Year. The celebrations begin on the first day of the lunar calendar and stretches throughout the month. A host of activities takes place during this time. It includes the preparation of special food, a send-off ritual for the Kitchen God, hanging of New Year paintings and spring couplets at home, letting off fireworks, visiting friends and relatives, giving out hongbao 红包 (small red paper packets with money for good luck inside), watching the lion dance, going to a lantern display, etc. Each of these activities holds a different meaning and collectively, they give the spring celebrations its all-embracing quality.

Besides historical acknowledgement and the popularity they enjoy, the main reason why Chinese festivals have become a tradition is because they evolved from a common practice of the people in society.

Some of these festivals may have started out as agricultural events devoted to a particular purpose. But as time went by, they became a custom and took on a multipurpose quality. The festive activities became richer in content and strengthened the life-force of these festivals, making them deeply entrenched in Chinese society. The Qing Ming Festival, for example, is one of the 24 solar terms in Chinese calendar. In the beginning, it was purely an agricultural affair, but as time went on, it became a manifold event, merging with activities connected to the Cold Food Feast, ancestor worship and tomb sweeping. After the Cold Food Feast was dropped from history, people started to regard ancestor worship and tomb sweeping as the main activities of Qing Ming Festival. It is hardly surprising then that in a modern society like Singapore, the real beginnings of the Qing Ming Festival as an agricultural celebration are not known to many.

The Dragon Boat Festival is another tradition observed by Chinese and shares similar beginnings with the Qing Ming Festival. According to historians, it started off as a practice in Wu Yue region in China to drive away evil and epidemics. Over time, it became a day devoted to the memory of historical figures like Qu Yuan 屈原 and Gou Jian 勾践, and incorporated entertainment and sporting activities like dragon boat racing which turned the festival into an all-encompassing event. With the development of history and transformation of society, traditional Chinese festivals are bound to face greater tests and challenges. *Origins of Chinese Festivals* is written and illustrated in a light-hearted manner to introduce readers to the significance of traditional festivals and their colourful and interesting activities. As renowned Chinese author Lu Xun 鲁迅 had put it: the spirit of a nation is the most precious; it is only through the development and enhancement of this spirit that a country can truly advance.

Traditional Chinese festivals embody the spirit of the Chinese and its cultural features. Understanding the significance of these festivals gives us a clearer picture of the roots of Chinese culture and thus helps us to appreciate what makes the Chinese stick as a race throughout their long history.

Dr Lee Cheuk Yin
Senior Lecturer
Department of Chinese Studies
National University of Singapore

About the Illustrator

Fu Chunjiang 傅春江 , born in 1974, is a native of Chongqing municipality in southeastern China's Sichuan province. He has been fond of drawing ever since childhood and graduated in Chinese language studies. Fu loves traditional Chinese culture and has tried his hand at drawing comics. Since 1994 he has been drawing comics and his works include *The Story of Kites* 纸鸢记 and *The Faint-Hearted Hero* 胆小英雄. He has also participated in the production of *One Riddle For One Story* 一个故事一个谜·

About the Translator

Koh Kok Kiang 许国强 is a journalist by vocation and a quietist by inclination. His interest in cultural topics and things of the mind started in his schooldays. It is his wish to discover the wisdom of the East that has kindled his interest in Eastern philosophy. He has also translated other titles in Asiapac Comic Series, namely *Book of Zen, Origins of Zen, Sayings of Lie Zi, Sayings of Lao Zi, Sayings of Lao Zi 2, Sayings of Zhuang Zi 2, Roots of Wisdom, Thirty-Six Stratagems, The I Ching, Yue Fei* and *The Eight Immortals*.

Introduction

The Chinese people have a history of 5,000 years of civilization. As a result, in the celebrations of important life events such as births and weddings, there are many customs. Information about these customs reflect the everyday habits of the Chinese, their traditions and mythological stories. They also reflect Chinese values such as loyalty and filial piety. This is also the case with Chinese festivals.

Some of the Chinese traditional festivals originated as far back as the Shang (1600-1100BC), Zhou (1100-256BC) and Han (206BC-AD220) Dynasties. Others appeared later, during the Tang (AD618-907) and Ming (AD1368-1644) Dynasties. In the course of social development, the customs and habits of the Chinese underwent gradual changes. The original meaning of some festivals became forgotten as they acquired new religious colouring or came to commemorate historical personages or events for ideological or political reasons.

Originally many of the festivals had their roots in the changes of the seasons because regular weather changes were vital in an agricultural society which China was and to a large extent still is. But gradually the plebeian origins of these festivals became obscure.

Depending on which philosophy or religion enjoyed imperial patronage or was in vogue during a particular dynasty, certain festivals became associated with particular beliefs or religions. Confucianism, Taoism and Buddhism have for long been regarded as the "three beliefs" of the Chinese people. Throughout history, advocates of the three beliefs have contended to win the hearts and minds of the masses.

For example, Qing Ming 清明 reflected the Confucian virtue of venerating ancestors. It is not surprising that the two stories associated with Qing Ming in this book took place during the Han Dynasty when Confucianism became the state creed. The Dragon Boat Festival 端午节 is another example of Confucian influence. It was originally aimed at propitiating the River God as the earliest traces of Chinese civilization can be found in the valleys of the two of China's longest rivers, the Yellow and the Yangtze Rivers. But by the time of the Han Dynasty, the festival came to be associated with Qu Yuan, a loyal official of the state of Chu during the Warring States Period (475-221BC). This is not surprising since loyalty is regarded as one of the cardinal Confucian virtues.

Taoism got into the act too. The story of Madam White Snake was originally a Taoist tale aimed at poking fun at Buddhism (the Buddhist monk Fa Hai is depicted as a wrecker of happiness) but somehow it came to be associated with the Dragon Boat Festival.

An example of a festival which took on religious colouring is Zhong Yuan Jie 中元节 on the 15th day of the seventh month. Originally it was a day of remembrance of ancestors. But after Buddhism entered China from India and became popular, the festival came to be associated with the Buddhist story of Mulian saving his mother.

Sometimes festivals took on a political flavour. For instance, the most common story associated with the eating of mooncakes during the Mid-Autumn Festival 中秋节 is that of how the Mongols of the Yuan Dynasty (1271-1368) were overthrown to make way for the Ming Dynasty (1368-1644). The new dynasty was eager to win the support of the masses and associated this story with the popular Mid-Autumn Festival.

Some festivals became intertwined with myths, such as the Qi Qiao Jie 乞巧节 (Plea for Dexterity Festival which is also known as Lovers' Festival). The Chinese have always been proud of their long period of culture and civilization and the association of major festivals with well-known myths acted as a sort of social glue that kept the people together.

The observance of festivals in China was also to ensure harmony and continuity. In old China, besides a number of relatively minor festivals, there were six major festivals in one year, known in the popular parlance as Three for the Living and Three for the Dead. The former were the Chinese Lunar New Year, Dragon Boat Festival and Mid-Autumn Festival while the latter grouping consisted of Pure Brightness Festival 清明节 (Qing Ming), the Festival of Hungry Ghosts 中元节 (Zhong Yuan Jie) and Shao Yi Jie 烧衣节 (Burning of Clothes Festival) which was celebrated on the first day of the tenth month, for sending winter clothes to the ancestors. This last festival has become uncommon.

Wherever there are Chinese, their festivals continue to be observed. But because of progress and the gradual shedding of ethnic traditions for modern and universal ways, many Chinese are no longer able to tell how their festivals originated. This is especially true of Chinese communities outside their homeland.

Koh Kok Kiang

Contents

Prologue  序言

The Chinese people have a history of 5,000 years and they have many traditional practices in the celebration of important life events. These practices either arise from the needs of everyday living or from folktales handed down from generation to generation.

In this age of technological advancement and information explosion, we live in an ever-changing world. As family size is getting smaller, the generation gap is now getting wider. The younger generation may not understand the origins of these traditional and customary practices. To bridge the gap, we now present folktales of traditional festivals through comics to help the younger generation to have a better understanding of the rich cultural heritage of the Chinese people.

Lunar New Year
农历新年

Lunar New Year is the most important Chinese festival. In the course of history it has been known by other names such as Time of the Beginning (Yuan Chen), First Day (Yuan Ri), First Day of the First Month (Yuan Shuo), Beginning of the Month (Yuan Zheng) and First Morning of the Year (Yuan Dan). Now it is known as the Spring Festival 春节 (Chun Jie) in China. It is a time for reunion and also represents renewal of the spirit. In the old days the common people lived frugally and New Year's Day was one of the few days when they could feast on delicacies.

The Story of Nian
年的故事

Tradition has it that a long time ago, the earth was full of venomous snakes and ferocious beasts. Among them was a huge creature called Nian 年. On the night of Lunar New Year's Eve, it would emerge to devour people.

Grrr!

5

7

Come with me. I'll show you my prowess.
I'll beat you to death!
Sawk!
We can't remain here with Nian on the rampage.
Whizz!

10

Dear villagers, Nian is most terrified of red. From now on, each house must paste red paper on the front door to prevent Nian from coming to wreak havoc.

Swish!

That old man must be some kind of a god.

Since then, the people had started to paste red paper on their front doors before New Year's Day. Later, the people wrote auspicious words on the paper which became couplets.

Origin of Spring Couplets
农历春节贴春联

A long time ago in the East China Sea, there was a mountain jutting out of the ocean called the Peach Capital Mountain. On the mountain grew huge peach trees and each of them had a big rooster on top. Each time the first rays of the sun broke through the darkness, the big roosters would start crowing, and this would rouse the roosters in each household into action.

Chonk!

The demons on the mountains are gnawing at the peach trees. I order you, Shen Tu 神荼 and Yu Lei 郁垒, to nab them to safeguard the peach trees.

That's the mountain below.

13

14

Heh! Heh! No demons would dare come here any more.

Shen Tu and Yu Lei stood guard day and night below the peach trees and no hungry ghosts and demons dared to go there to eat their fill. Since then people have regarded Shen Tu and Yu Lei as the kings in charge of all the ghosts and demons.

17

Pasting of Door Gods on New Year's Day
除夕贴门神

The custom of pasting pictures of guardian gods on doors began in the Han Dynasty. It was only from the Tang Dynasty onwards that generals Qin Shubao and Yuchi Jingde who served under Emperor Li Shimin became the guardian gods.

*the third of the five two-hour periods into which the night was formerly divided

After Wei He subdued the Dragon Lord, that night the Dragon Lord came to disturb the emperor.

Return my life to me!

Argh! It has been like this every day. I will soon no longer be able to take it any more.

Your Majesty, do not fret.

We, Qin Shubao and Yuchi Jingde, will stand guard outside your bedroom door to protect you from evil spirits.

25

Keeping Brooms out of Sight on Lunar New Year's Eve 除夕藏扫帚

According to tradition, a long time ago there was a merchant named Ou Ming who travelled by boat to do business. One day he arrived at Lake Pengze.

There's going to be a storm!

Floop!

Splosh!

The boat was carried by the strong waves to an island.

28

29

31

Hanging of Red Lanterns
过年挂红灯龙

Towards the end of the Ming Dynasty, the rebel "Dashing King" Li Zicheng and his men fought their way to Kaifeng.

Dashing King, if we don't invade the city, we'll soon run out of provisions.

37

What can we do if he enters the city at night and kills the wrong people in their homes?

That's true. That won't be good.

I have an idea. We can put a small red lantern in front of our homes.

Whether it is day or night, if the Dashing King sees the red lantern, he will know that it is a poor household.

I will pass on this information to Li Zicheng in the form of a letter.

But you must not let the rich people and treacherous officials know about this.

39

Come here! Save me! I'll give you money!

Those boats have red lanterns. This one doesn't carry any.

Splish!

Come back! Come back!

Aiyah! The red lanterns are actually a sign of identification.

Eek!

Even having money is no use!

To commemorate the Dashing King's rescue of the common people, the Chinese henceforth like to hang red lanterns on auspicious occasions such as the New Year.

Waving the Dragon Lanterns 舞龙灯

Tradition has it that in Zhejiang province's Jinhua county, there is a Mount Qiling. At the foot of the mountain is a famous Lingxi stream.

The people used the water from the Lingxi stream to irrigate their land.

43

A snake that likes to eat grain products is rare indeed.

The days passed quickly.

That summer was very hot and the water in the stream was drying up.

44

46

48

49

50

Letting off Bamboo Firecrackers
过年放炮竹

According to tradition, on the top of a hill full of bamboo grove lived a group of strange creatures called Mountain Beings. They were not more than a foot tall and had only one leg.

55

56

First Day of the New Year

正月初一

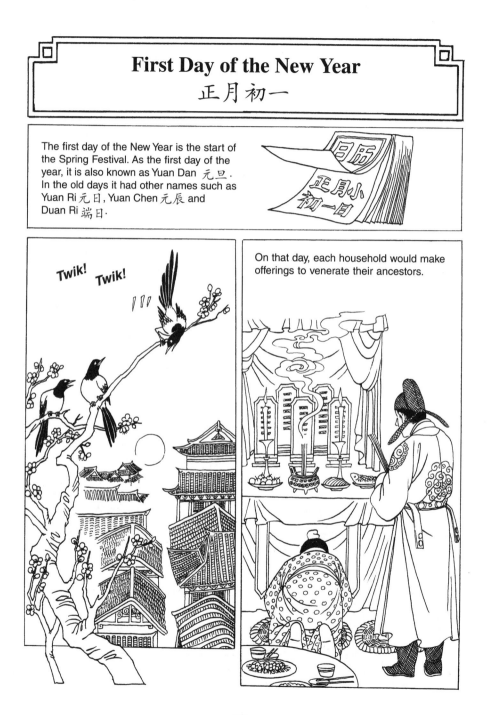

The first day of the New Year is the start of the Spring Festival. As the first day of the year, it is also known as Yuan Dan 元旦. In the old days it had other names such as Yuan Ri 元日, Yuan Chen 元辰 and Duan Ri 端日.

Twik! Twik!

On that day, each household would make offerings to venerate their ancestors.

On that day, some families would put the ancestral tablets on the altar.

Some people offer incense to the ancestral portraits.

After praying to their ancestors, according to customary practices, they would walk out of their doors in an auspicious direction to move around.

The west is considered an auspicious direction.

When walking out of their doors, they would carry lanterns and let off firecrackers.

Brrak!

After that they would arrange offerings to the God of Happiness.

59

Everybody would move in the auspicious direction...

This is the tenth temple we are visiting!

On the way, if they came across any temple, they must go in and burn joss sticks to pray for a good year ahead.

The people also let off firecrackers to drive away illnesses and to wish for peace and security.

The most common activity on that day is Bai Nian 拜年 or making visits. It is also called Zou Chun 走春 or Tan Chun 探春.

Wish you happiness and prosperity.

Same to you.

If a prominent person has too many relatives and he is unable to visit all of them, he would send his name card or send them a fu 福 (prosperity) character.

New year greetings, grandfather!

The person offering the greetings would be given yasui money 压岁钱.

Rise. Here's a red packet for you.

Greetings to your company. Please give our company your support.

In the Ming Dynasty and Qing Dynasty palaces, the practice of group visits to offer New Year greetings was popular and it also spread to the rest of society. Nowadays, such practices are still followed.

Same to you. Thank you for taking the trouble to come.

Second Day of the New Year
正月初二

The second day is also a day for making visits. In addition, it is a day when married women return to their maiden homes to renew their ties with their parents, brothers and sisters.

The most distinctive activity on that day is to attract the God of Wealth into homes. Each home would display pictures to "attract wealth and draw in treasures".

At night families would float lights on the rivers.

Third Day of the New Year
正月初三

Some people regard the third day as the "loyal dog day" and these people would not go out or receive visitors.

Today I'm free and at leisure.

On this night, lanterns must not be lit late in the night and grain and salt must be scattered on the floor of the house.

This is to feed the rats.

People must go to bed early.

Turn in early. Don't bother the rats who are making merry.

Tee! Tee!

Among the common people, tradition has it that the night of the third day of the New Year is when rats get married.

63

Fourth Day of the New Year
正月初四

The fourth day of the New Year is the day for attracting the deities from the heavenly to the earthly realm. But the ceremony must be held after noon.

Brraak!

Offerings include incense and food, and firecrackers are also let off. Pictures of the deities and their guards are burnt to invite them to earth.

Fifth Day of the New Year
正月初五

The fifth day is also known as Po Wu 破五 or Breaking the Five. After this day the people can bring the trash out to be disposed of.

I am the one to do it again.

It is also a day to remove offerings. The people look at the weather on that day to determine whether it will be a peaceful year ahead.

The weather is clear today. Looks like it will be a peaceful year ahead.

I pray to the palace of the gods for good fortune and prosperity.

The fifth day is also the birthday of the gods of the five directions. Businesses make offerings of cloth to the gods and hang red cloth in front of their premises.

The Seventh Day is Day for Human Beings 正月初七是人日

According to Chinese tradition, a long time ago heaven and earth was like an egg-shaped mass.

Pan Gu盘古, the mythical ancestor of the Chinese race, was inside it. His body was 90,000 li* long.

One day, he woke up.

* One li is equivalent to half a kilometre

66

Pan Gu broke open the egg with tremendous force. The less dense part of it became the sky and the heavier part became the earth.

It will no longer be joined as one again.

But heaven and earth kept drawing closer and Pan Gu had to use his arms to hold up heaven and his feet to push down earth. After tens of thousands of years, the sky and earth became thicker and could no longer join together again. Pan Gu was so exhausted that he laid down and died.

Huff!

After Pan Gu's death, his left eye became the sun and his right eye became the moon. His body became the mountains and his blood the rivers, his hair became the vegetation and his sweat the rain and mist. His entire body was used up.

A long time later, a female deity named Nü Wa 女娲 came to this world.

What a lonely place this is!

I only have the reflection of myself in the water for company.

69

Eighth Day of the New Year
正月初八

The eighth day is a day of paying homage to the stars. Hence the people pray to the god of the stars.

At night offerings are made to the stars.

Other activities include attending temple fairs ...

viewing flowers ...

and going on excursions to high places.

Ninth Day of the New Year
正月初九

Yuan Xiao Festival
元宵节

Yuan Xiao Festival
元宵节

During the reign of Emperor Wu Di of the Han Dynasty Dongfang Shuo was strolling in the imperial garden.

In this place, I'm the only one who appreciates you.

77

78

80

81

82

83

84

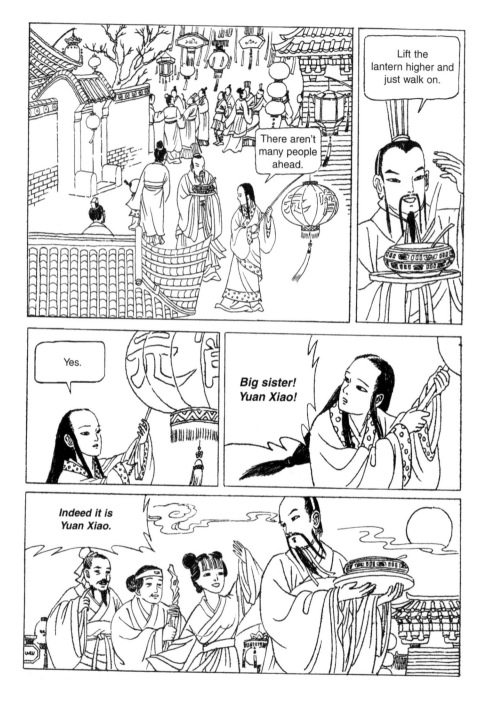

* Glutinous rice balls are called Yuan Xiao in northern China and Tang Yuan in southern China.

87

Cold Food Day
寒食节

In olden times, Cold Food Day was a very important festival. It was usually the day preceding Qing Ming. The most famous story related to Cold Food Day is that of Duke Wen of Jin and Jie Zitui 介之推 .

During the Spring and Autumn Period (770-475 BC), Duke Xian of Jin was enamoured of his second wife Li Ji.

Li Ji slandered his first wife and her sons and the duke made Li Ji's son his successor.

The eldest son committed suicide.

The second and third sons, Zhonger and Yiwu, fled into exile.

91

My achievement today is due to the help from all of you.

Somebody has submitted a memorial.

This memorial is about Jie Zitui. Why have I forgotten about him?

Zhonger eventually returned to Jin and became the ruler with the title of Duke Wen. He rewarded all the officials who followed him into exile but forgot about Jie Zitui.

My son, I've heard that people have been unfair to you. What do you plan to do?

94

95

97

Swoosh!

The fire on the mountain raged for three days and nights before it burned itself out.

Your Highness, leave here quickly!

98

Duke Wen made clogs from the wood of the tree where the two bodies were found to remind himself of Jie Zitui. He also renamed Mount Mian as Mount Jie in memory of Jie Zitui.

He also ordered that henceforth on this day in the state, no fire must be lit to cook food and the custom became known as Cold Food Day.

Qing Ming Festival
清明节

According to tradition, the name Qing Ming started in the Han Dynasty because the weather during the third month of the year was clear and pure. It was only during the Tang Dynasty that it became a festival. The custom of sweeping tombs then became prevalent.

Scattering of Five-Coloured Paper
坟上压五色纸

During the struggle preceding the establishment of the Han Dynasty, Liu Bang was helped by able officials and later took the throne as Emperor Gaozu.

Clong!

103

A great wind rises,
Clouds fly and scatter,
With power over the
four seas, I return to
my homeland.

Oh!

I'll still remember my hometown after my death.

I only lament that my parents cannot share in my good fortune.

This place has seen the chaos of war. Do you people know where my parents are buried?

The tombstones in the graveyard are damaged and the engravings are no longer distinct. I'm afraid ...

105

Swish!

The papers have floated there.

Indeed it is my parents' grave.

Father! Mother! Your unfilial son is back.

Since then, when people clean graves during the Qing Ming Festival, they make sure that the surroundings are clean and place five-coloured paper at the tombstone to signify that the descendants are praying and showing respect to the deceased.

Flying Kites During Qing Ming
清明节放风筝

Qing Ming falls in the third lunar month. In springtime, the air is clear and pure.

Because the wind direction is not constant after Qing Ming, the practice of kite-flying is only followed until Qing Ming.

Besides showing respect to the dead on this day, people make excursions to the countryside. One of the activities which one never fails to see is kite-flying.

According to tradition, during the Warring States Period the philosopher Mo Zi built a wooden hawk after three years of efforts.

Soar!

Swish!

Look! That toy is flying in the sky and is not falling down.

Oh, it is a pity that this invention is not passed on to the descendants.

Don't tell me that I, General Han Xin, is no match for the ancients.

Surely it can fly with this design.

110

111

112

113

114

The things that flew that night were an invention of Han Xin. It was a paper hawk that could emit a sound like a zheng or zither-like instrument. In the old days the paper hawks could make sounds. Hence they came to be known as feng zheng 风筝.

Xiang Yu was cornered at the river bank and he committed suicide.

Dragon Boat Festival

端午节

Commemoration of Qu Yuan
屈原的故事

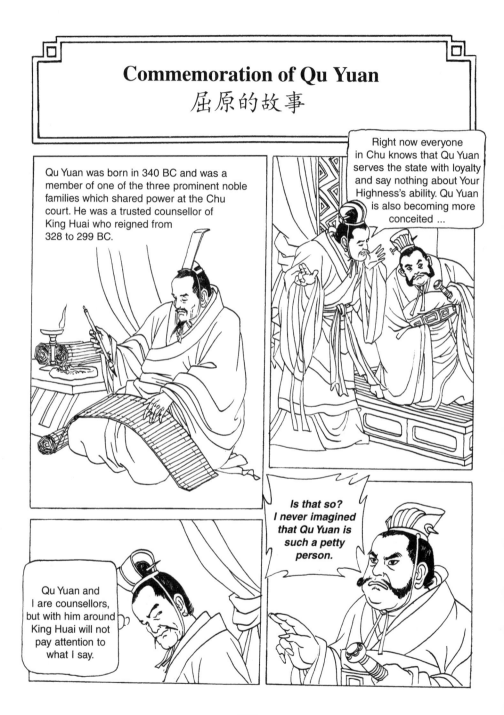

Qu Yuan was born in 340 BC and was a member of one of the three prominent noble families which shared power at the Chu court. He was a trusted counsellor of King Huai who reigned from 328 to 299 BC.

Right now everyone in Chu knows that Qu Yuan serves the state with loyalty and say nothing about Your Highness's ability. Qu Yuan is also becoming more conceited ...

Qu Yuan and I are counsellors, but with him around King Huai will not pay attention to what I say.

Is that so? I never imagined that Qu Yuan is such a petty person.

An alliance between Qin and Chu ended when Qin declared war on Chu and seized parts of its territory. In the midst of the fighting, Qin proposed that the Chu monarch go to Qin for ceasefire talks.

We entreat the King of Chu to attend the talks in person.

Seems like it will be a worthwhile meeting.

Qin is a rapacious state which cannot be trusted. It is better for you not to go.

Father, as Qin is the most powerful state, we cannot afford to offend it in any way.

Zi Lan is your son as well as my student. His words should carry more weight than Qu Yuan's.

All right, I think I will go after all.

King Huai was taken captive after he arrived in Qin and died 3 years later in prison.

The eldest son Qing Xiang became king and Zi Lan was made premier. Zi Lan slandered Qu Yuan and Qu Yuan was banished from the capital.

If only my state had heeded my advice, the king would not have come to such a plight.

During this time Qu Yuan composed the famous poem Li Sao.

In the year 278 BC, the Qin army occupied Chu's capital Ying.

121

123

124

125

Dragon Boat and Cao-e
划龙舟与曹娥

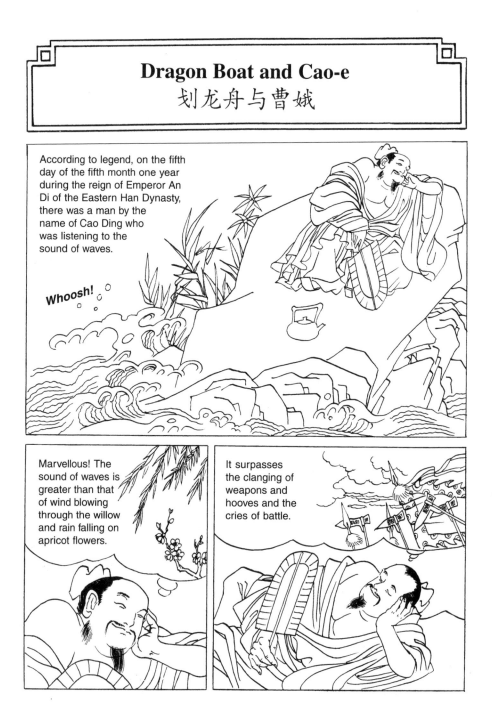

According to legend, on the fifth day of the fifth month one year during the reign of Emperor An Di of the Eastern Han Dynasty, there was a man by the name of Cao Ding who was listening to the sound of waves.

Whoosh!

Marvellous! The sound of waves is greater than that of wind blowing through the willow and rain falling on apricot flowers.

It surpasses the clanging of weapons and hooves and the cries of battle.

128

129

Madam White Snake
端午话白蛇

The story of Madam White Snake has long been associated with the Dragon Boat Festival.

It is said that there were two snakes in the heavenly realm who transformed themselves into women and came to Hangzhou, the paradise on earth.

This was during the Song Dynasty.

Boatman, please ferry me. I'll pay you

131

132

133

134

135

137

139

141

142

143

145

The Chinese Valentine's Day

七夕：中国情人节

The seventh day of the seventh lunar month is the Chinese Lovers' Day or Valentine's Day. The most popular story mentioned in connection with this festival is that of the Cowherd and the Weaving Girl.

The Cowherd and the Weaving Girl
牛郎织女七夕会

149

151

157

159

161

163

Whizz!
Countless magpies formed a bridge.
Ah! A bridge of magpies!
In that case, I will allow you two to meet on the bridge of magpies on the seventh day of the seventh month every year.
Grandmother, don't go back on your words!

Since then on the seventh day of the seventh month, people pray to the Cowherd and the Weaving Girl.

I pray for everlasting youth and beauty.

I pray for a pair of deft hands.

During the Northern and Southern Dynasties Period, women would thread a special needle at this time.

The needles had seven holes. To complete threading it was a sign of merit.

Look, I've completed threading it!

Me too!

During the Song Dynasty, women would put a spinning spider into a small box.

The next morning, they would open the box and see if the spider had spun a web. A well-spun web would signify that they had achieved merit.

166

During the Ming and Qing Dynasties, women would float a needle on the surface of the water in a bowl.

They would then look at the image reflected at the bottom of the bowl. If the image showed things such as flowers, birds or beasts, then it meant that the needle would be productive.

Married women would also buy a Moheluo clay doll on this day in the hope of giving birth to a child.

Because the Moheluo doll often carried a lotus leaf, children playing in the streets also carried a lotus leaf on this day.

Zhong Yuan Festival 中元节

In olden times the 15th of the first month, the 15th of the seventh month and the 15th of the tenth month were known as the Three Yuan. Since olden times the Chinese have believed that during the first to the 30th day of the seventh month, the gates of hell are opened and hungry ghosts wander on the earth.

Originally Zhong Yuan Festival was a day of remembrance of ancestors, but after Buddhism was introduced to China the festival took on a Buddhist flavour and became known as Yu Lan Pen Jie 盂兰盆节 . Yu Lan Pen has long been thought to be the Chinese transcription of the Sanskrit term Ullambana, and in Chinese it means "to be suspended upside down".

However, French scholar Jean Przyluski has said Yu Lan Pen is probably not a transcription of Ullambana, but rather of Avalambana, a term which seems to have been applied in India to certain meritorious offerings made to the whole living community, through which benefit might be acquired for the dead. This would indicate that the festival has Indian origins.

The term Yu Lan Pen is associated with Buddhism. On Zhong Yuan Festival each Buddhist temple forms a Yu Lan Pen Society which lights lanterns and recites sutras so as to lead those in hell across the sea of suffering.

According to the Buddhist sutras, the Buddha once commanded Mulian (Maudgalyayana, one of the Buddha's disciples), because his mother had been reborn among the Hungry Ghosts in hell where she was not allowed to eat anything, to form a Yu Lan Pen Society. On the 15th day of the seventh month the society would put all kinds of different-tasting fruits into basins, and offer them so as to nurture great virtues in the ten quarters - the eight compass points, and above and below.

The Buddhist emperor Liang Wudi of the Liang Dynasty was responsible for popularising the observation of Zhong Yuan among the masses.

Mulian Saves His Mother and the Yu Lan Pen Society

目连救母与盂兰盆节

171

Mid-Autumn Festival 中秋节

The Mid-Autumn Festival revolves around the moon and there are many traditional stories concerning the moon. It is believed that the Mid-Autumn Festival originated more than 2,000 years ago and in the old days the festival was devoted to praying to the gods. Because China is largely an agricultural society, the 15th day of the eighth lunar month happens to occur after the autumn harvest. That day the sky is generally clear and the weather fine and the people celebrate with post-harvest feasts, signifying the principle that "the divine and the human are one". During the Song Dynasty, due to the influence of learned people, praying to the moon became widespread. The eating of mooncakes started towards the end of the Yuan Dynasty because of a folk story of that time and later the observation of the Mid-Autumn Festival became important.

Gazing at the Moon Till the Fourth Watch
赏月到四更

177

178

179

181

A golden loom!

It's really made of gold!

How can this be?

Sixth Sister Yao, what did you do last night?

Last night, first the oil lamp ran out of fuel, then a dragon boat appeared from the moon. There was a strong wind and after that I could not do any more work.

Don't tell me this is just as it is described in traditional lore.

My dear daughther-in-law, it was wrong of me to treat you like this. In future I won't beat you. You are a blessed person. Let's share weal and woe.

During mid-autumn night, immortals would leave the moon palace on a dragon boat. For those who are lucky enough to see them, whatever they touch would turn into gold.

They lived harmoniously ever after.

The story was passed down and the custom of gazing at the moon until the fourth watch became prevalent. It is said that the custom is based on the hope of seeing the dragon boat.

The Story of Chang-e
中秋话嫦娥

It is said that during the time of the legendary Emperor Yao, there were ten suns which took turns to illuminate the earth.

Ah! There are ten suns.

Puff!

But one day, out of playfulness the ten suns appeared together in the human realm.

One sun brings prosperity to humanity, but ten suns spell doom.

186

188

189

190

Presenting of Mooncakes during the Mid-Autumn Festival 中秋送月饼

193

194

195

196

Later, to commemorate the joyous occasion of getting their liberty and peace, the people would eat the cakes during the Mid-Autumn Festival. The cakes underwent constant changes before they evolved into the mooncakes of today with many different fillings.

Chong Yang Festival 重阳节

The ninth month is when the chrysanthemum blossom, and the ninth day of the ninth month is called Chong Yang Festival. It is also called Chong Jiu 重九 (Double Nine). In ancient times, on this day people would climb hills to view the scenery. Everybody would drink chrysanthemum wine and pluck dogwood leaves and fruit. They would fill a red silk gauze with dogwood leaves and tie it to their arms. It is said this would help prevent calamities.

In actual fact, during late autumn the weather becomes unconducive to health. Vegetation starts to wither and it is easy for pestilence to occur. In places where there are a lot of people, it is easy for people to fall sick. Hence climbing hills is not only a pleasurable activity, it can also help people to avoid pestilence. Dogwood and chrysanthemum have been used by people since ancient times for their medicinal properties. Dogwood is said to be good for preventing pestilence while chrysanthemum can be used to treat a great variety of ailments. It can also help promote longevity.

The story about Climbing Hills on Chong Yang Festival took place during the Han Dynasty.

Climbing Hills on Chong Yang Festival
重阳节登高

201

203

207

209

210

211

After that the people did not suffer pestilence any more. To commemorate Huan Jing's slaying of the demon, the people continued the practice of ascending hills on the nine day of the ninth month.

213

Dong Zhi 冬至
(Winter Solstice Festival)

Many people think that Dong Zhi means the "arrival of winter". In fact what Dong Zhi means is that after this day the sunshine will decline. In the northern hemisphere, the day is the shortest during Dong Zhi. In the southern hemisphere, it is the reverse.

During the New Year everybody would make visits. In olden times, during Dong Zhi the people would also make visits. Some people would offer incense at dawn and some businesses would take a break on that day. People would feast and the atmosphere was just like the New Year. In China, because the onset of winter was cold and medical science was not advanced, at this time of the year many people froze to death. As a result, on this day people would gather together to eat tang yuan 汤圆 (glutinous flour balls). Yuan 圆 (round) is associated with tuan 团 (reunion) and yuan 圆 (complete). Eating tuan yuan is therefore symbolic of family unity and harmony.

216

217

219

Getting recognition is a great feeling. I'm happy. I can work with zest.
Same here.
Time for your meal.
I feel hungry earlier than usual.
I was so engrossed in my work.
Let's see what good stuff we are eating today.
How come there's no food?
This is uncooked grain. Do you know how to cook?
I only know how to shape metal.
I only know how to lay bricks.
I only know how to ...
Since cooking is nothing special, cook the food by yourselves.

220

221

A Brief Chronology of Chinese History

夏 Xia Dynasty			About 2100 – 1600 BC
商 Shang Dynasty			About 1600 – 1100 BC
周 Zhou Dynasty	西周 Western Zhou Dynasty		About 1100 – 771 BC
	東周 Eastern Zhou Dynasty		770 – 256 BC
	春秋 Spring and Autumn Period		770 – 476 BC
	戰國 Warring States		475 – 221 BC
秦 Qin Dynasty			221 – 207 BC
漢 Han Dynasty	西漢 Western Han		206 BC – AD 24
	東漢 Eastern Han		25 – 220
三國 Three Kingdoms	魏 Wei		220 – 265
	蜀漢 Shu Han		221 – 263
	吳 Wu		222 – 280
西晉 Western Jin Dynasty			265 – 316
東晉 Eastern Jin Dynasty			317 – 420
南北朝 Northern and Southern Dynasties	南朝 Southern Dynasties	宋 Song	420 – 479
		齊 Qi	479 – 502
		梁 Liang	502 – 557
		陳 Chen	557 – 589
	北朝 Northern Dynasties	北魏 Northern Wei	386 – 534
		東魏 Eastern Wei	534 – 550
		北齊 Northern Qi	550 – 577
		西魏 Western Wei	535 – 556
		北周 Northern Zhou	557 – 581
隋 Sui Dynasty			581 – 618
唐 Tang Dynasty			618 – 907
五代 Five Dynasties	後梁 Later Liang		907 – 923
	後唐 Later Tang		923 – 936
	後晉 Later Jin		936 – 946
	後漢 Later Han		947 – 950
	後周 Later Zhou		951 – 960
宋 Song Dynasty	北宋 Northern Song Dynasty		960 – 1127
	南宋 Southern Song Dynasty		1127 – 1279
遼 Liao Dynasty			916 – 1125
金 Jin Dynasty			1115 – 1234
元 Yuan Dynasty			1271 – 1368
明 Ming Dynasty			1368 – 1644
清 Qing Dynasty			1644 – 1911
中華民國 Republic of China			1912 – 1949
中華人民共和國 People's Republic of China			1949 –

SPECIAL OFFER

Strategy & Leadership Series

☐ Chinese Business Strategies
☐ Three Strategies of Huang Shi Gong
☐ Six Strategies for War
☐ Sixteen Strategies of Zhuge Liang
☐ Thirty-six Stratagems
☐ 100 Strategies of War
☐ Gems of Chinese Wisdom

Make your subscription for any 5 volumes or more of this comic series (tick box) and enjoy **20% discount**.
Original Price: S$15.90 per volume (*exclusive* of GST)
Offer at special discount (*inclusive of* postage):-

	5 Volumes	6 Volumes	7 Volumes
Singapore	68.30	82.20	95.30
Malaysia	71.60	88.30	101.00
International-by sea mail	78.60	100.30	113.00

* All Prices in Singapore Dollars. 3% GST charge for local orders.

I wish to subscribe for the above-mentioned titles

at the nett price of **S$**_____ (*inclusive of* postage)

☐ **For Singapore orders only:**
Enclosed is my postal order/money order/cheque/ for **S$** _____

(No.: _____ .)

For Singapore/Malaysia/International orders:

☐ Credit card. Please charge the amount of SIN$_____ to my credit card

VISA ☐ Card No. _____ Card Holder's Name _____

MASTER ☐ Expiry Date_____ Order Date_____ Signature _____

Name _____

Address _____

_____ **Tel** _____

Send to: ASIAPAC BOOKS PTE LTD 629 Aljunied Road #04-06 Cititech Industrial Building
Singapore 389838 Tel: 65 -7453868 Fax: 65 -7453822
Note:
For this offer of 20% discount, there is no restriction on the titles ordered, that is, you may order any 5 or more of the series. Prices are subject to change without prior notice.

CHINESE MYTHS & LEGENDS

The Most Enthralling Chinese Tales in Comics

IN SEARCH OF DEITIES	Wang Xuanming
THE HEADLESS TRIBES	Wang Xuanming
CHINESE TALES OF THE SUPERNATURAL 1	Wang Xuanming
THE EIGHT IMMORTALS	Chan Kok Sing
LEGENDS OF JI GONG: Reincarnation of an Arhat	Chan Kok Sing

Offer for Local Readers:

Original Price for one set of five volumes   **S$53.67** (*inclusive of* GST)
*Special price for one set of five volumes   **S$48.30** (*inclusive of* GST)

> ## Send this complete page for your mail order

I wish to order _____ set(s) *of Chinese Myths & Legends*
at the nett price of S$48.30 per set.

Enclosed is my postal order/money order/cheque No. _____

for S$ _____.

Name _____   **Tel** _____

Address _____

_____ Singapore _____

Send to: ASIAPAC BOOKS PTE LTD 629 Aljunied Road #04-06 Cititech Industrial Building
         Singapore 389838 Tel: 7453868 Fax: 7453822

Note: Prices are subject to change without prior notice.
Offer is for readers in Singapore only.

SPECIAL OFFER

LIVING 21 SERIES - A powerful new comic series to equip you with timeless principles to be successful and effective in the 21st century.

1. **Chinese A.R.T. of Goal Setting**
2. **Chinese T.A.C.T.I.C.S. in Negotiation**
3. **Chinese Art of Leadership**
4. **Chinese Art of Excellence**
5. **Chinese Art of Team Building**
6. **Chinese Art of Commitment**

Make your subscription for this new comic series and enjoy **10% discount**.

Original Price for 6 volumes: **S$79.72** (*inclusive of* GST)

Special price for subscription of 6 volumes: **S$71.75** (*inclusive of* GST)

I wish to subscribe for _____ sets of *LIVING 21 SERIES* at the nett price of S$71.75 per set.

Enclosed is my postal order/money order/cheque/ for S$_____ (No.: _____)

Name (Mr/Mrs/Ms) _____ Tel _____

Address _____

_____ Fax _____

Please charge the amount of S$ _____ to my VISA/MASTER CARD account (only Visa/Master Card accepted)

Card No. _____ Card Expiry Date _____

Card Holder's Name (Mr/Mrs/Ms) _____ Signature _____

Send to: ASIAPAC BOOKS PTE LTD 629 Aljunied Road #04-06 Cititech Industrial Building
Singapore 389838 Tel: 7453868 Fax: 7453822

Note: Prices subject to change without prior notice. Valid for orders in Singapore & Malaysia only. Each volume will be mailed to you upon publication. Delivery of all 6 volumes to be completed by December 1997.

SPECIAL OFFER

Romance of the Three Kingdoms Vols. 1-10 in a NEW DISPLAY BOX!
China's Greatest Historical Classics in Comics

**FREE: 216-page comics entitled "Sixteen Strategies of Zhuge Liang".
Free delivery.**

Offer for Local Readers:

Original Price for 10 volumes	**S$99.91** *(inclusive of* GST)
*Special price for whole kit	**S$97.00** *(inclusive of* GST)

Send this complete page for your mail order

I wish to order _____ set(s) *of Romance of the Three Kingdoms* **Vol. 1-10**

at the nett price of S$97.00 per kit.

Enclosed is my postal order/money order/cheque No. _____

for S$ _____

Name _____ **Tel** _____

Address _____

_____ Singapore _____

Send to: ASIAPAC BOOKS PTE LTD 629 Aljunied Road #04-06 Cititech Industrial Building
Singapore 389838 Tel: 7453868 Fax: 7453822

Note: Prices are subject to change without prior notice. **Offer is for readers in Singapore only.**

<< 亚太漫画系列 >>

中国节日的故事

编著：吴珮琪

绘画：傅春江

翻译：许国强

亚太图书有限公司出版